THE LEPRECHAUN
LIBRARY

# MYTHICAL BEASTS

Deirdre Headon
Illustrated by Alan Baker

HUTCHINSON
London Melbourne Sydney Auckland Johannesburg

# THE BASILISK

The basilisk was the most deadly of all creatures, for a single glance from its yellow, piercing toad's eyes would kill both man and beast. Its power of destruction was said to be so great that sometimes simply to hear its hiss could prove fatal.

Said to have been hatched out of a cock's egg after it had been incubated by a toad for nine years, the basilisk never grew longer than two feet. Indeed, it is hard to believe that this small snake-like creature could have been so deadly. The markings on its forehead, which looked like a crown, led some people to call it the King of Serpents, and its breath was so venomous that it caused all vegetation to wither. Although it preferred to live in hot, dry climates, it is more likely to have lived surrounded by a desert of its own making.

There was, however, one creature which could withstand the basilisk's deadly gaze, and this was the weasel. No one knows why this was so, but although the fierce weasel could slay the basilisk, it would itself be killed in the struggle.

Perhaps the weasel knew the basilisk's fatal weakness: if it ever saw its own reflection in a mirror it would perish instantly.

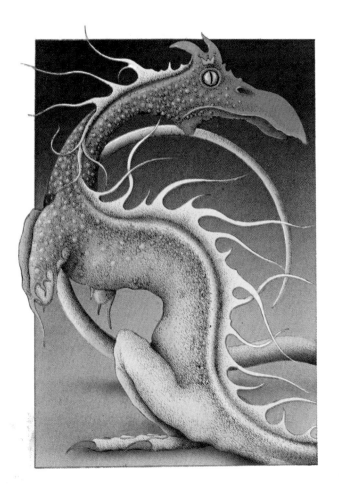

# THE ANT-LION

The ant-lion is one of the most fantastic creatures described in medieval bestiaries, having the foreparts of a lion and the hindquarters of an ant. This curious creature's form resulted from its having a lion for a father and an ant for a mother.

It was not long-lived, for this 'thing of two natures' could eat neither grain (due to its father's nature) nor meat (due to its mother's nature). This conflict meant there was no food suitable for it.

However, modern scholars of theology would like us to believe that the ant-lion is a pure creature of the imagination which grew out of a mistranslation in the Bible. They argue that in the Book of Job an archaic Greek word for lion was mistranslated. What should have read 'the old lion perisheth for lack of prey' appeared in an early translation of the Bible as 'the ant-lion perisheth for lack of prey'.

# THE GRIFFIN

High on barren mountain-tops, perched on nests lined with gold, griffins jealously guarded their vast hoards of gold and jewels. The golden brightness of their treasure made men associate the griffins with the sun itself, and they were said to draw the chariot of Apollo, the sun god, across the skies. However, only a foolhardy man would attempt to steal their treasure, for although he might succeed in reaching a griffin's nest he would almost certainly, once there, be torn to pieces by the beast's great claws.

The greed and rapaciousness of the griffin was legendary, and on one occasion it led to their downfall. A twelfth-century account of a voyage to China describes how some sailors dressed themselves in animal skins, as protection against the stormy weather. Some griffins, spying these tasty-looking morsels on the deck, swooped down and carried them off to their nests. Once the griffins had deposited their prey safely in their nests, the sailors burst out of their protective skins and slew the astonished griffins. Hardly believing their good fortune, the sailors quickly made off with the griffins' fabulous treasure.

The claws of these hybrid monsters – part eagle and part lion – were much sought after, for they were highly prized as drinking cups. Moreover, it was believed that if the claw were dipped in a drink it would reveal whether or not the draught was poisoned. One so-called griffin's claw brought back from the Crusades may be seen today in the cathedral in Brunswick.

# THE LEVIATHAN

The leviathan, undoubtedly the largest monster in creation, was said to be so massive that only the oceans of the world were large enough to contain its vast bulk. As this indestructible monster wallowed through the deeps its eyes gleamed strangely, and an eerie light shone from its mouth making the surrounding water bright with a hoary light. Its voracious appetite was legendary: it was capable of eating, in a single gulp, sea serpents three hundred leagues in length.

In Jewish legend, after God had created the universe He realized that the enormous power, strength and appetite of the leviathan jeopardized the rest of His creation. As He had fashioned only two such monsters He destroyed one so that the race could not be continued. However, to ensure that His marvellous skill in creating the leviathan should not vanish without trace, God is said to have made the remaining leviathan immortal.

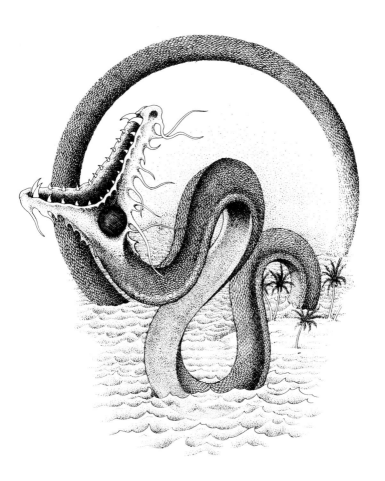

# THE MINATOUR

Bull-men are found throughout the world's mythology but the most brutal was the Minatour of Crete. Having the head of a bull and the body of a man, the Minatour was famous for its unbridled strength and savage cruelty. It lived at Knossos in a vast labyrinth built by Daedalus for King Minos. The king could not bear the sight of the monster, to which his wife Pasiphae had given birth after an unlawful union with a bull. This bull had been sent from the sea by Neptune as a sign of his power. When Minos had failed to sacrifice the bull, the vengeful sea god had made Pasiphae fall in love with it.

The Minatour fed from human flesh, provided by means of a macabre ritual. Every nine years, seven youths and seven maidens would be sent from the city of Athens to be thrown into the Minatour's labyrinth. Minos's justification for demanding this awful tribute was that some years earlier his son had gone to Athens to take part in the games, and the Athenians, jealous of his physical prowess, had slain the youth.

Eventually, Theseus came to the Athenian's aid, determined to slay the Minatour. Minos's daughter Ariadne, who had fallen in love with him, advised Theseus what to do. He entered the labyrinth armed with a sword given to him by Ariadne – and a ball of string. Ariadne had told Theseus that by leaving a trail of string he would avoid getting lost in the maze. Eventually, he succeeded in killing the Minatour and finding his way out of the maze. His mission accomplished, Theseus and Ariadne sailed joyously away from the island.

# THE AMMUT

There can be no doubt that the creature the ancient Egyptians feared above all others was the Ammut, a monster who had the head and jaws of a crocodile, the body of a lion and the hindquarters of a hippopotamus. The reason they so feared it was because this savage beast devoured the hearts of all men found unworthy to enter heaven.

The Ammut stood in the Hall of the Two Truths next to the scales of judgement, manned by the jackel-headed god Anubis. When a man died his spirit had to prove before forty-two deities that he was worthy to enter heaven by denying that he had lived a sinful life. The spirit would swear that he had not killed any man; used false weights, caused hunger or stolen any offerings to the dead. The final judgement on his claims was reached when Anubis weighed his heart (symbolizing the actual deeds of his life) against a feather (symbolizing the truth of his words). If the scales did not balance, Anubis would swiftly toss the heart to the Ammut who waited open-jawed to devour any sinful man's heart.

Fortunately Egyptians who had studied *The Book of the Dead* could escape the gruesome attentions of the Ammut for this book laid down all the correct responses a spirit could make to ensure his entry into heaven.

# AREOP-ENAP

On the island of Nauru in the South Pacific, Areop-enap, the giant spider, created the world.

In the beginning Areop-enap was the only living creature journeying through limitless space. During his wanderings he came upon a vast, rounded clam-shell but he could not find its opening. After making an incantation he succeeded in opening its lid just enough to squeeze inside. Its interior was very dark and there was so little space that he could not stand upright in the shell.

As he crawled round, he found a horn-shaped shell. Enfolding it in one of his legs he slept with it against him for three days, thus instilling it with magical powers. He then asked the creature in the shell if it could raise the clam's lid a little to let in light. This the creature did, whereupon Areop-enap took him and placed him in the western part of the clam where it formed the moon.

Finding another, larger, horn-shaped shell, he endowed it with the same magic, at which the shell's creature raised the clam's lid even higher. Areop-enap then placed it in the eastern part of the shell to form the sun.

Now having enough light to see clearly, he spied a caterpillar who, with great effort, raised the clam's lid completely, his sweat forming the sea. It is the lower part of the clam-shell which forms the earth and the upper half the heavens.

# THE CYCLOPES

The Cyclopes were an undisciplined race of giants. The distinguishing feature of a Cyclops was that it had only one eye, which glared from the centre of its forehead through a mane of thick dark hair.

The lazy, lawless Cyclopes were also man-eaters, but the Greek hero Odysseus got the better of one Cyclops, Polyphemus. Stranded on an island in the Aegean Sea, Odysseus and his crew took shelter in Polyphemus's cave where he lived with his flock of ewes. On his return the Cyclops promptly devoured two of the crew. Odysseus, unable to endure the giant's threats of what lay in store for the remaining crew, offered Polyphemus some wine. The wily Greek continued to ply him with drink until the Cyclops fell down in a drunken stupour. Straight away Odysseus made a pointed stake out of the trunk of an olive tree, and, with the aid of his crew, drove the stake into the comatose Cyclops's single eye.

Mad with anger and pain, the blinded Polyphemus rose up and blocked the entrance of the cave. But Odysseus devised an ingenious escape plan. He and his men each tied themselves to the under-belly of one of Polyphemus's ewes when the giant sent them out of the cave to graze the next morning.

When he realized the Greeks had escaped, the enraged Polyphemus fumbled his way to the top of the island's cliffs. The last sight the Greeks had as they sailed away was of the Cyclops hurling rocks into the sea at random in the hope of sinking their ship.

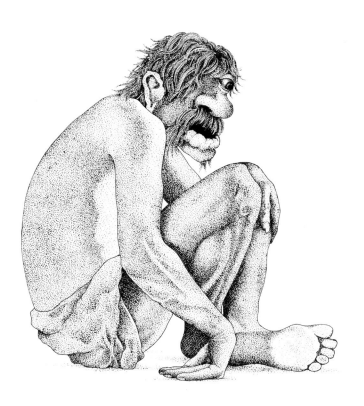

# ———THE WESTERN DRAGON———

In the West the dragon was the natural enemy of man. Although preferring to live in bleak and desolate regions, whenever it was seen among men it left in its wake a trail of destruction and disease. Yet any brave attempt to slay this beast was a perilous undertaking. For the dragon's assailant had to contend not only with clouds of sulphurous fumes pouring from its fire-breathing nostrils, but also with the thrashings of its tail, the most deadly part of its serpent-like body.

However, dragons were not without their own fears. According to one authority, the dragon had only to hear the flapping of an eagle's wings to rush into hiding. The sight or shadow of the 'perideus' tree would also make the dragon turn tail, for the dragon could not tolerate its sweet-smelling fruit. This is why doves, a favourite food of dragons, often took refuge in the branches of this tree.

Nevertheless, some dragons were reported as having a strangely sentimental side to their nature – they were susceptible to beautiful maidens. One lovesick dragon was so distressed when it found the object of its affections loved a youth instead that it is said to have resorted to gently chastising her on the legs, but it would on no account harm her.

# CERBERUS

Cerberus was the monstrous triple-headed dog who guarded the entrance to Hades, the underworld. This hell-hound passed his time greeting the newly-arrived souls of the dead with a flick of his serpent's tail. At the same time he would terrify them by barking loudly and snapping his wide jaws.

Cerberus's temperament and appearance made him a very efficient guard dog, who also revelled in his task of preventing souls escaping from hell. Any unfortunate soul who was fool enough to try to escape from the underworld was liable to be torn to pieces by Cerberus's razor-sharp teeth. However, it was believed that Cerberus could be pacified and made as gentle as a lamb if pieces of honey cake were placed in each of his three mouths.

It is not surprising to discover that this beast did not like daylight. One of the ten labours of the Greek hero Hercules was to bring Cerberus up to the light of day. Securing the beast with mighty chains of iron, he dragged the raging dog up into the sun. Cerberus, made mad by the light, filled the air with flecks of white foam from his three mouths. On touching the ground the foam was transformed into the poisonous flower aconite.

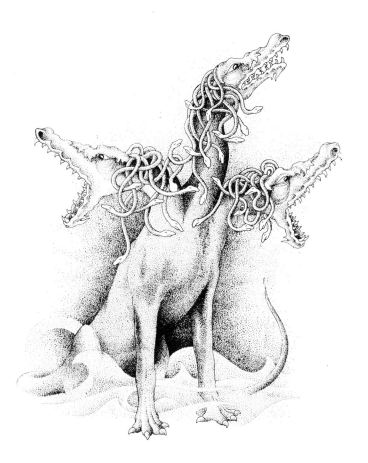

# THE FENG-HWANG

In ancient China the feng-hwang, a bird of paradise, was a bird of good omen. It had the head of a pheasant and the body and resplendent plumage of a peacock. As it flew it was accompanied by flocks of lesser birds and the sound it made was said to cause the crops to flourish and the trees to grow.

To receive a visit from the feng-hwang was to be looked on favourably by the gods, and if the bird visited the Emperor's garden it meant that the ruler's reign was just. No celebration was felt to be complete unless the feng-hwang graced the festivities with its presence. Its appearance at a wedding was considered especially auspicious, for the bird was believed to symbolize perfect love.

However, the Chinese, not always trusting the whim of the gods, believed there were certain ways to ensure a visit from the feng-hwang. This bird could always be persuaded to come into a garden in which a 'hu tung' tree grew, as this was its favourite habitat. The feng-hwang was also very susceptible to sweet music. The sound of the lute was an allurement which the bird could not resist.

Sadly, these dazzling and benevolent creatures were not long-lived. But it is said that when a feng-hwang died, a hundred birds of the air would peck a hole in the earth so that it could be properly buried.

# THE CACTUS CAT

During the last century travellers through the great cactus-growing regions of Tucson in the United States would sometimes witness the nocturnal antics of the lunatic cactus cat.

Though the size and shape of a normal cat, it differed in that it had thorny hair, which was especially prickly on its ears. Its tail was branched and held rigid, and upon its forearms and front paws were sharp, knife-like blades of bone.

With these blades the cactus cat would make a systematic round of all the largest cacti in the area, slashing the base to free the sap. This procedure could take several days for the cactus cat was most meticulous in seeking out only the best plants. By the time it had worked its way back to the first cactus, the sap would have started to ferment. The white sticky sap would by now be a sweet and very intoxicating liquid. After lapping up the sap greedily the cactus cat would soon become very drunk.

Often the inebriated cactus cat was said to be heard rasping its bony forearms together and screeching with delight as it waltzed off into the moonlight.

# THE TENGU

The tengu was the most troublesome creature of Japanese legend. Part bird and part man, with a red beak for a nose and flashing eyes, the tengu was notorious for stirring up feuds and prolonging enmity between families. Indeed, the belligerent tengus were supposed to have been man's first instructors in the use of arms.

Many believed the main cause of the tengus' disruptive behaviour to be that they longed for men to revere and worship them. For this reason tengus particularly liked to plague Buddhist priests, who always appeared to the tengus much adulated, and people eventually grew to believe that priests who had lived wicked lives became tengus.

Once, on a journey, a Buddhist monk saw a procession of priests whom he recognized as his dead Buddhist brothers. They seemed much as they had been in life except that their eyes flashed and their noses seemed longer and redder. But the monk did not take in these warning signs.

The monks sat down and took turns to drink from a golden cup. No sooner had they done so than they began to writhe in agony, and smoke and flames rose from their heads. Yet within a short space of time they returned to normal. The priest realized that these were no longer monks but tengus, and that what they had drunk was hot metal – a thrice-daily torture to which tengus were condemned as punishment for their sins.

# YOUWARKEE

On a mysterious island in the South Pole lived a race of flying people known as 'glumms', who were never seen during the day as the sun's light hurt their eyes. The glumms flew by means of a feathered covering called a 'graundee' which extended down their backs and along the outsides of their arms and legs. When a glumm raised his arms the graundee would open out like a fan, enabling him to fly. The graundee was also waterproof, and when tired of flying glumms enjoyed nothing more than floating on their backs in water.

A female glumm was called a 'gawry', and the most beautiful of them all was Youwarkee. Her body was covered with soft silky down and glowed the palest pink colour, and as she flew her graundee fanned out to make her look like a Venus emerging from a shell.

One day Youwarkee damaged her wings while practising somersaults during flight. She was rescued and revived with madeira wine by Peter Wilkins, an eighteenth-century Cornish sailor whose ship had been drawn off course by the island's magnetic force. Wilkins immediately fell in love with Youwarkee, and after a makeshift marriage ceremony, the couple lived together in great happiness for many years. Youwarkee would often fly errands for Wilkins, and he made dresses for her to wear. He even made her some spectacles so she could go out in the sun.

Sadly, Youwarkee died, but the glumms helped Wilkins to make his way back to England where he told of his marvellous adventure.

# THE SQUONK

During the last century lumberjacks working in the forests of Pennsylvania would lighten the dark evenings by telling of the 'fearsome critters' who lived in these forests. The squonk was one such creature, but it was not as fearsome as it would have liked to appear.

The squonk was a shy and elusive creature, more often heard than seen for it was constantly weeping. It wept because it was very self-conscious and unhappy with its appearance. It is easy to see why. First, this cumbersome creature had a very ill-fitting skin which hung in ugly folds and was also covered with warts and moles. Its face was not a pretty sight either, being swollen from continual weeping; for the same reason, its eyes were puffy and red-rimmed.

One man tried to catch a squonk, and was delighted when he finally managed to do so. By imitating the call of a female squonk he tricked the gullible creature into jumping inside a sack. Confident that he now possessed the only squonk in captivity he returned home. But when he untied the sack he discovered all that remained of the squonk was a puddle of tears and a few watery bubbles.

# THE BANSHEE

The fearful wailing of the banshee, heard at the dead of night, was said to be the most mournful sound on earth, for it signified that someone close to the hearer was about to die. If more than one banshee was heard wailing it presaged the death of some great personage.

In Ireland some believed the banshee – a Celtic fairy – to be the spirit of a young woman who had died in childbirth. Others thought she was the spirit of a virgin who had died young returning to warn her family of the imminent death of a close relative. Any person courageous enough to venture out when the banshee was abroad might catch sight of her veiled wraith-like figure crouched beneath trees crying bitterly.

However, in Scotland the banshee assumed a more monstrous appearance. Her eyes were ringed with red from continual weeping and through her long streaming hair one fang-like tooth emerged beneath her single nostril. She was found lurking by water washing the shrouds of those about to die, and was believed to have webbed feet.

But the banshee could also bring good fortune to men. If someone crept up behind the weeping banshee as she was at her washing, and placed a hand on her shoulder, he could claim a wish from her.

# THE UNICORN

Men have always sought the elusive unicorn, for the single twisted horn which projected from its forehead was thought to be a powerful talisman. It was said that the unicorn had simply to dip the tip of its horn in a muddy pool for the water to become pure. Men also believed that to drink from this horn was a protection against all sickness, and that if the horn was ground to a powder it would act as an antidote to all poisons. Less than 200 years ago in France, the horn of what was believed to be a unicorn was used in a ceremony to test the royal food for poison.

Although only the size of a small horse, the unicorn was a very fierce beast, capable of killing an elephant with a single thrust from its horn. Its fleetness of foot also made this solitary creature difficult to capture. But Leonardo da Vinci, who made a special study of the unicorn, wrote that it could be tamed and captured by a maiden. Made gentle by the sight of a virgin, the unicorn could be lured to lay its head in her lap, and in this docile mood, the maiden could secure it with a golden rope. The maiden would then turn the captured beast over to the hunters, who would slay it.

In the Middle Ages, this hunt, betrayal and destruction of the unicorn was seen by men to symbolize the Passion of Christ. Others saw in the maiden/unicorn relationship the pure and chaste love of a knight for his lady. However, in China the unicorn was regarded as a more consistently gentle beast, for the unicorn took infinite care, as it walked, not to trample a single tiny creature underfoot.

# MEDUSA

Among the most terrifying females in Greek mythology were the Gorgons. Originally beautiful maidens, the goddess Athene changed the three sisters into bird-like monsters after one sister, Medusa, had slept with Poseidon, god of the sea. The goddess not only made them hideous, with huge teeth, glaring eyes, lolling tongues and serpent locks, but caused any man who dared to glance at them to turn immediately into stone.

However, Medusa was not completely transformed, for though she had serpents' hair and a bird's form she retained her beautiful face. This made her the most deadly of the sisters as she seduced men with her looks, luring them to her with the sweetest-sounding voice. Indeed, the ground beneath her perch was littered with the stone figures of her unfortunate victims.

Eventually Perseus succeeded in killing Medusa. Armed with the shield and sword of Athene and wearing Hermes' winged sandles, he managed to cut off her head by looking not at her but only at her reflection in his shield. He presented the head to Athene and its image was incorporated for ever more in the goddess's shield.

# THE CHINESE DRAGON

The colourful Chinese dragon was a more benevolent creature than its Western counterpart. Rich beyond men's wildest dreams, dragons inhabited wonderful palaces of coral and gold in the sky, and as they climbed up to these dwellings their breath was said to form the clouds and the pressure of their feet on them to cause the rain. As they moved through the air the dragons' voices sounded like copper pans jingling in the wind.

Dragons enjoyed nothing more than cavorting around the skies, riding on the winds (often accompanied by swallows, their favourite playmates). Indeed, when in a playful mood they would often try to bite the sun. But though fun-loving, dragons were often capricious and vain. One emperor discovered this when he tried to draw a dragon king, for no sooner had the emperor put paint to paper than the affronted beast whipped up the most tremendous storm.

The dragon also enjoyed divine status in China for it was the creature who could span heaven and earth in a single leap. Early emperors were thought to be descended from dragon kings and the emperor was the only man with enough authority to make the dragon desist from disturbing the weather with its somersaults in the sky. Philosophers, too, sought their counsel for dragons were held to be the wisest creatures. It was for this reason that they were usually depicted holding a pearl, which symbolized their wisdom.

# THE PHOENIX

From ancient times the phoenix, the deathless bird of myth, has symbolized resurrection, for it is miraculously reborn from its own ashes once every five hundred years.

When the phoenix senses its death approaching, it flies back to the deserts of Arabia where it was born, and makes a pyre of branches from the frankincense and myrrh trees. It then mounts this pyre and, turning its body towards the sun, fans out its wings. As it rotates, its wings are ignited by the rays of the sun. The phoenix is consumed by the flames until all that remains are its ashes. But among the ashes is a worm, which emerges after nine days, as the new phoenix, resplendent with red and gold feathers.

In legend the first duty of the newly-born phoenix is to bury its 'parent'. It fashions an egg out of the ashes and carries it to the Egyptian temple of the sun at Heliopolis. Here the precious egg is guarded for ever more by the priests of the temple.

# THE DUN COW

Many centuries ago when giants still lived in England, people told tales of the great dun cow, which could be found grazing among the green pastures of the county of Shropshire.

This enormous red and white cow was a very docile creature with a generous nature. Her main claim to fame was that she provided an endless supply of milk which was used by the local giants and, in times of need, she would also allow men to take a share of her yield.

However, one day a witch decided to test the cow to see if her yield of milk was really endless. Using a sieve instead of a bucket, the witch continued to milk the cow through a whole day. As was to be expected, the sieve could not be filled and though at first the cow was oblivious to what was happening she eventually realized that her generosity was being abused. Thereupon she went berserk and rampaged through the countryside leaving a trail of injured people and trampled crops right into the nearby county of Warwickshire.

The gigantic cow caused so much destruction here that the local inhabitants were forced to call upon the aid of the local dragon-slayer, Guy of Warwick, to kill the demented creature.

# THE YAHOOS

The Yahoos were the most obnoxious and disagreeable beasts described in Lemuel Gulliver's celebrated account of his travels to remote parts of the world.

While journeying to the island of Madagascar, he arrived at an unknown land. Although armed with trinkets to offer as gifts to the natives, his composure was broken when he saw some strange creatures loping quickly towards him. They had hideous flat faces with wide mouths, and their heads and breasts were covered with hair, some lank, some frizzy. Their beards were like those of goats, and they had a long ridge of hair (brown, red, black or yellow) extending down their backs and on to the front of their legs and feet. The rest of their skin was bare and flesh-coloured.

Terrified by the sight of Gulliver, for they had never seen a man before, these deformed yet timid creatures nimbly climbed, with their clawed feet, up into a high tree. As Gulliver looked up at the babbling creatures they proceeded to shower him with excrement.

Gulliver's first unfavourable impression of the Yahoos was soon confirmed by the more gracious inhabitants of the island, the Houyhnhnms. They could not, however, tell Gulliver where the Yahoos came from, but what was certain was that they were prolific breeders. Their unsocial habits had posed such a threat to the civilized and rational Houyhnhnms that they used the Yahoos as beasts of burden; a state of servility in keeping with their foul nature.

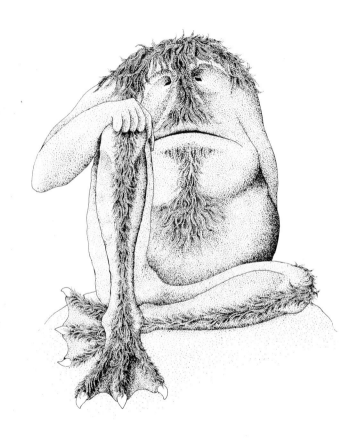

# MÉLUSINE

The mermaid is one of the most bewitching creatures of legend, with the beautiful face, golden hair and torso of a woman set above a fish's tail. Mermaids longed to win the love of a mortal man for only through such a union could they gain an immortal soul.

This is seen in the tragic tale of the captivating French mermaid Mélusine. Forsaking the river where she had been born she assumed human form and won the love of Raymond, nephew of the Duke of Poitiers. They married, but every Saturday Mélusine would mysteriously disappear, for on this day she would secretly take a ritual bath which enabled her to maintain her human form. She was anxious that her husband should not see her while in her true form, for if he were to do so she would return to her fish-woman shape for ever more.

For many years Raymond did not question his wife's weekly disappearance, but eventually his curiosity got the better of him. One day he spied on his wife in her bath and discovered she was a mermaid. Realizing her trust had been betrayed, Mélusine immediately fled from the castle, abandoning her children and her husband.

However, it is said that every night she returned to her children's nursery to watch over them as they slept. People were often said to have seen her there, lit by the moonlight, her golden hair gleaming and the blue and white scales of her fish's tail shining smooth and glossy as enamel.

# THE SCIAPODS

The sciapods were first described by the Greek poet Lucian, who wrote an account of travels to fabulous countries. There were different types of sciapods but they all had a common and distinguishing feature: one enormous foot. This was used to provide shade and sciapods were sometimes better known as the foot-shade men.

Having only one foot was no hindrance to their mobility and they were reported to be capable of hopping so fast that no one could catch them. According to a description found in a German bestiary, they could reach an even greater speed when leaping on the sea.

Sciapods found in the East were known as monoscelans. A very fierce and brave race, they were well adapted to the hot countries they inhabited. They had three small feet so that their large foot could be used as a shade while they continued walking.

All sciapods lived on the fragrance of fruits and trees and for this reason they never set off on a journey without carrying something to smell. However, it was said that if they smelled anything more pungent than the scent of roots, trees and wild apples, it could prove fatal to them.

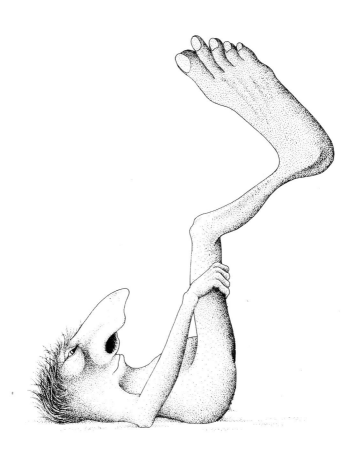

# PEGASUS

Pegasus was the winged horse created by Neptune from sea and sand mingled with the blood of the slain Gorgon, Medusa. He possessed all the grace of a perfect, finely-bred horse and his large, strong wings were capable of bearing him right up to the gates of heaven.

He could often be found drinking the waters of the Pierian fountain, the source of poetic inspiration in ancient myth. For this reason Pegasus was often regarded as a symbol of inspired poetry.

It was here that the hero Bellerophon found Pegasus when he sought his aid in slaying the monstrous Chimera. Pegasus willingly allowed Bellerophon to ride on him and by flying at a great speed Pegasus easily out-manoeuvred the clumsy Chimera, allowing Bellerophon to kill the monster. But Pegasus was a modest creature and would take no credit for the major part he had played in this conquest.

However, Pegasus did not go unrewarded by the gods. Rising up to the heavens he was allowed to take a place among the stars, where his winged shape can still be seen outlined in the night sky.

# THE MONSOK

Many centuries ago, voyagers to the Southern Ocean brought back descriptions of a marvellous race known as the monsok. These creatures walked on two legs, had eight digits on their hands and feet and sometimes had tails. But they were most memorable on account of their gigantic ears.

Some observers reported that they resembled the ears of the female elephant and reached down to the creature's knees. However, others were said to have such large ears that they reached down to the ground. Their ears did not impede their mobility and men who saw them described how a monsok was adept at wrapping each ear around an arm, pushed well up to the elbow. Once this was done the monsok could continue on its way.

The monsoks, sometimes simply called the ear-men, put their ears to good use as they provided an excellent ready-made protection against inclement weather. Also, being a nomadic race, the monsoks' large ears made their lives much easier in that their wanderings were not determined by where they could find shelter at night. A monsok could stop just where it wanted and wrap its ears around its body to keep itself warm and dry throughout the night.

# THE KRAKEN

In the past, mysterious islands have often risen from the depths of the sea, in the deep waters which surround Scandinavia. Once a bishop landed on one such island to celebrate Mass. But as he sailed away from the island he was astonished to see it disappearing beneath the water. It seems that the island had, in fact, been part of a great tentacle of the monster known as the kraken.

It is not difficult to see why the bishop should have made this mistake: this giant sea squid reached a length of one-and-a-quarter miles, and portions of its massive green legs breaking the surface could easily be mistaken for islands. Besides its vast legs, which created whirlpools when they broke the surface, it had great horns which emerged like ships' masts from beneath the sea. The creature was also omniverous, and so strong that it could crush a ship by simply coiling a tentacle around its bulk. The vessel would then be dragged to the bottom of the sea where the kraken would devour it.

The kraken was a constant threat to sailors who soon came to know if it was slumbering in the waters beneath them, because the depth of the sea would suddenly diminish. Discovering this ominous sign, sailors would hoist their sails and as quietly as possible leave the shallow waters, hoping to escape before the kraken awoke.

# ———ACKNOWLEDGEMENTS———

Of the many books which have provided source material for *Mythical Beasts* the most valuable were:
*A Dictionary of Fabulous Beasts,* Richard Barber and Anne Riches (Macmillan, 1971)
*The American People,* edited by B.A. Botkin (Pilot Press, 1948)
*Fabulous Beasts,* Peter Lum (London, 1952)
*The Book of Beasts,* T.H. White (Hogarth Press, 1954)

Hutchinson & Co. (Publishers) Ltd
An imprint of the Hutchinson Publishing Group
3 Fitzroy Square, London W1P 6JD

Hutchinson Group (Australia) Pty Ltd
30-32 Cremorne Street, Richmond South, Victoria 3121
PO Box 151, Broadway, New South Wales 2007

Hutchinson Group (NZ) Ltd
32-34 View Road, PO Box 40-086, Glenfield, Auckland 10

Hutchinson Group (SA) Pty Ltd
PO Box 337, Bergvlei 2012, South Africa

First published 1981

Designed and produced for Hutchinson & Co. by
BELLEW & HIGTON
Bellew & Higton Publishers Ltd
19-21 Conway Street, London W1P 6JD

Copyright © Bellew & Higton Publishers Ltd 1981
ISBN 0 09 145560 X

Printed in England